Socialism: A Growing Malignancy in America
by W. E. Schmidt
© 2007

First Printing December 2007

ISBN: 1-4196-9777-3
EAN13: 978-1-4196-9777-7

For ordering information, write to
R. Nation
P.O. Box 834
Astor, FL 32102

Table of Contents

Introduction

Modern liberalism in America today is really socialism rising in influence. Throughout history, the socialist agenda has been to place all social planning in the hands of the government and minimize or eliminate private enterprise. Today's American Liberals also strive to increase the power of government by taking responsibility out of the hands of the people and centering it in the hands of politicians and bureaucrats. Wittingly or not, as the Democratic Party has become more liberal, it has become the New Socialist Party of America.

Liberal Democrats believe that their philosophy is a "progressive" one, filled with promise and social completeness. And too many Americans are falling for this groundless fantasy. In reality, this movement would ultimately strip Americans of their freedoms; cripple free enterprise, resulting in subsistence living (as it did in Soviet Russia); contort the original intentions of the Constitution; and erode the bedrock of society, the family unit.

The chapters that follow sound the alert that if we don't cut out this growing malignancy called socialism, we'll lose the freedoms and prosperity that makes our nation so great.

I. Socialism and Industry

Chapter 1
A Classless Society:
Neither Classless Nor Equal

In any society, injustices and inequalities occur. If man's flawed nature is the cause, who's got the solution?

Socialism seeks to control all aspects of socioeconomic development and so eliminate class distinctions to make everybody equal. But what does this perspective of equality mean? It means there would be equal status among the general population, while the politicians and bureaucrats held positions of power. The result is a two-class America: a working class relegated to mandatory "equalized" subsistence living; and a government class whose members make all the decisions for everybody. The reason? Socialist idealism contends that people cannot make decisions in the best interest of the common good due to such weaknesses as dishonesty and greed. However, there is one big hole in the ship of this philosophy: the bureaucratic class would *also* consist of imperfect human beings. Therein the real temptation exists to pass laws that benefit the lawmakers at the expense of the populace. The politicians and bureaucrats, then, become the chosen few who can get what they want, not just what they need.

By contrast, a democratic America has a multi-class society. The spectrum stretches from the poor who have little, to the middle class who enjoy a limited mix of necessities and nonessentials, to the rich who have lots of everything. This is the way of free enterprise. Our country does not guarantee equality of wealth, just equality of opportunity. There is no limit to our aspirations if we have the will to pursue a better way of life. Wealth is won and lost through good luck or bad, endeavor or indolence, but no one is relegated to one class from birth until death.

At this point a modern American Liberal might say that we must control business to reduce the injustices caused by man's worst qualities. Unfortunately, this action would evolve into the nationalization of natural resources, basic industries, banking and credit, and public utilities.

With bureaucracy established as permanent management over industry, it would not have to prove financial responsibility to the law or society in the same way that private enterprise does. In this situation, poor management and profit shortfall would become too easily remedied by raising taxes. (For examples, look at the histories of Amtrak, the U.S. Postal Service, or NASA.) Ultimately, nationalization becomes a financial parasite of the people, accelerating rather than slowing poverty and unemployment.

Therefore, a government that fosters free enterprise–even factoring in human weakness–will inspire the most good. Three benefits come to mind. First, as an objective viewer, government watches out for injustice rather than perpetrating it. Second, government provides the freedoms sufficient for the generous expression of some of humanity's *best* qualities: individual talent, ambition, compassion, and cooperation. (It's worth noting here that under free enterprise, even selfish motives can have positive consequences. Example: A greedy businessman, despite himself, may provide goods or services that benefit mankind.) And third, without deliberate planning by appointed centralized sources, the aggregate genius of millions of citizens, entrepreneurs and business leaders bring about economic wisdom, diversity, and reasonably balanced decisions that together provide society with the means to attain much beyond mere subsistence living. Poverty is less prevalent and more temporary. Wealth and economic stability are more available, and so more attainable by all. That's equality.

Chapter 2
Let Good Business Be

What degree of control should government exert over enterprise? Americans have seen the irresponsible zeal to maximize profit result in corporate scandal, fraud, and general corruption. At these times, Liberals step forward and demand more government involvement in business. At best, they are like the Socialist idealists before them who believed they could be better, do better and quash bad business practices. At worst, they are just as power and profit hungry as the corporate thieves they claim to cleanse. Assuming that the Liberals' motives are pure, what harm could more government involvement in business possibly do?

Plenty. Above all, it would unravel a system that is predominantly good, and overwhelmingly working. Free enterprise is the driving force in our economy. Though large businesses may exert pressures on the economy as a whole, small business is the fabric of American enterprise. The entrepreneurialism of myriad small businesses accounts for the majority share of America's wage earners. They play a large part in the stability of our economy by spreading wealth, risk, and opportunity among many. It is practically impossible (and hideously expensive) for government to get involved in minutia at such levels. Even if such involvement were possible, it would handicap the fluid movement of goods and services and turn the process into a complex maze.

Big business then, one might say, could be better managed by the government. After all, those huge operations affect everyone's lives. But that's the reason big business should be left unencumbered to do what it does so well already. It is through its large industrial capabilities and resources that big business is able to meet the demands of an ever growing population and economy. Big business' ability to meet cash requirements for major capital investments in technology and production usually cannot be met by smaller entities. Because of this, however, more responsibility is placed on these larger businesses to look out for the socioeconomic needs of their country.

Profit for the sake of the stockholder and top management reward must be weighed against the well being of not only the employees in their organization but society as well. To isolate oneself as a business dedicated only to the bottom line at the expense of ethics will inevitably result in destruction of public opinion, customer alienation and a call for more government control; all strong deterrents. And yet excesses occur.

So what should government's role be in business? Certainly not actual involvement, for that would snarl into micromanagement of the worst kind. Instead, a free-enterprise democracy protects its citizens best by enforcing *the existing laws* that apply to fraud, corruption, employee abuse, black marketing, organized crime, discrimination, and monopolistic ploys, among others. That's right, the laws already exist. So government's role should be limited to oversight and enforcement. Liberals who indiscriminately push for more laws would better invest their time joining with others to review existing laws to increase enforcement and raise fines and penalties. (Even serious white-collar crimes should be punishable to the point of life in prison without parole.) Otherwise the push for more laws merely becomes a push for government to consider more ownership of business. Americans must use their voting power to ensure that bad business is punished while good business remains to operate freely.

Chapter 3
More Taxes = Big Government
= Big Mistake

No country can exist without a tax structure to provide for the defense, infrastructure, and services necessary to ensure a stable and secure nation. The trick is to find a tax structure that is fair and just, which distributes the benefits of tax proceeds equitably and does so without waste and self-serving policies. While no taxing system is perfect, the one that does the least harm is the one that keeps taxes to a minimum. For an explanation, we can look at the two operating cultures in America.

First is the culture of citizens working in agriculture and private business that make products and services available to the general population. Employees perform their jobs and derive income from their contribution to the company and the way it satisfies the needs of the buying public. It is essential that the farm or company make enough profit to assure its future and provide for the needs of its owners, employees, investors, and creditors. A concern for the customers' best interests transfers to success for the enterprise and its workers. So, the wage of the private business worker ultimately depends on customer satisfaction.

The second culture of citizenry works for city, county or federal entities providing important civil services and enforcing the laws of the land. Revenues for supplies, services, and employee wages come not from the sales of goods or services, but from license taxes, fuel tax, sales tax, income tax, and other tax mechanisms as mandated by political or legislative decisions. The public servant has to work harder to maintain a discipline of compassion towards fellow citizens because the servant's "master" is government policy, and his or her wages are dependent on a pre-set budget.

While both private and public workers can perform necessary and valuable tasks, the characteristics of bureaucracy do not allow for the natural attrition of nonperforming staff, obsolete departments, or overspending. For example, failure to provide good and valued product or services in the private sector means employee termination and/or business failure. Failure in a bureaucracy means long-term administrative action to terminate, suspend, or transfer questionable employees. Programs or agencies that should be eliminated continue to operate or are absorbed into other departments. And as for the subject of spending . . .

How do bureaucracies that set strict budgets to provide a fair accounting to the citizens they serve wind up consuming huge amounts of tax revenue and then asking for more? First, if a department or agency spends under budget, two points of failure are assumed: Either the budget was not accurately estimated, or the intended mission was not attained. So, to make sure that no criticism is encountered in the use of tax revenue, department and agency heads mandate that all funds must be spent. End-of-year surpluses will not be carried over, but be taken away. Subsequently, there is often a mad rush at the end of the fiscal year to consume these funds, in wise fashion or not. And new-year budgets remain the same but more probably increase. It doesn't matter that a department and its employees were tenacious in holding down costs or operating efficiently. In fact, by default, efficiency and conscientious thrift are not rewarded in the bureaucratic arena. The public worker instead strives to satisfy their budget objectives while carrying out government policy. Huge amounts of tax revenue are consumed and rarely is there a surplus.

The second reason that more government begets more spending is that its employees derive their wages from tax revenue, and as a voting bloc of the population, will tend to vote for those candidates who enhance the size of government through taxation. More taxes makes more government. More government means more government workers exerting more influence in the legislative process to fund their agencies and increase their wages, a condition ripe for corruption. The nature of bureaucracy seeks to perpetuate itself until its members outnumber those in private enterprise. Eventually more and more employees become government employees and the culture of public worker spreads unchecked. In this work atmosphere the motivation is to serve the system, not the customer. History has shown that even after a country abandons socialism in favor of a free-market society, the corrosive work perspective of the former regime hinders the success of a fresh start.

We must not let that happen here. By resisting requests for tax increases, American citizens force government to look within itself for waste. Obsolete programs get cut. Inefficiency gets trimmed. Budget bloating, corruption, and misuse of funds are curbed. By restraining government growth, the culture of the public worker remains a necessary, but small, subset of the overall population–with pressure, competition, and example from the private sector keeping it in check–and therefore more apt to live up to the definition of public *servant* rather then self-serving bureaucrat.

Chapter Four
Labor Unions and Socialism

In general, unions are logistically desirable in big business to represent the larger work force in dealings with management. The union-employer relationship should be symbiotic one in which the health and wealth of both company and employee are adequately served. Unfortunately, even though the original intent of unions may have been just that, all too often they have veered away from the first two players in this relationship to serve a third: the union itself.

The horror stories are many: Union pension funds misused. Union-controlled money accounts misappropriated for union management's self-serving agendas. Employee issues used to make unreasonable demands and shield corruption and greed.

At other times, unions have proved overzealous in their defense of employee causes, often at the expense of the employee and the industry itself. Grievance committees which could be used as a useful tool to cooperatively navigate through changes in industry trends and technology, have instead been used to stifle innovation for fear that workers' jobs will be threatened. In reality, the long-term effect of modernization means job security.

Consider the plight of Michigan. There, auto industry unions made sure their workers were paid well, to the point of overpay. Due to competition and high cost, plants for production were shut down, moved, or contracted out of state or country. Workers were laid off. Some of those towns are now so depressed that homes sell for less than they are worth. Many people have left Michigan because they can't find work there. Those who remain can't sell their homes without taking a loss. Some homes are even abandoned. Those who still work in the auto industry don't dare leave because anything else would mean a drop in pay. How could it come to this? And why did the auto industry suffer such a dramatic change? The following history lesson will show that when American companies lose their competitive edge against foreign companies, they cease to operate or move out of the country.

At the end of World War II, industrialized Europe and Japan were destroyed. As a result, every bit of industry in those countries had to start from scratch, and the latest and most innovative means of production could be developed. By the late 1960s Japan had a burgeoning and modern steel-making capability. Meanwhile, the United States' steel-making industry was still using 1920s' and 1930s' technologies because the powerfully entrenched unions restricted any attempts at modernization for fear of loss of jobs. Americans watched as Japan's innovations produced steel more cheaply to supply its growing auto industry and to compete in the world steel market. The U.S. steel industry, weakened by these and other factors, couldn't compete and lost valuable market share. The term "rust belt" came into existence as steel mill after steel mill shut down or sold out.

Japan *did* become a key player in the auto industry, followed by the heavy equipment industry. Then, like the U.S. steel industry before them, American heavy equipment manufacturers like Caterpillar, John Deere, and International Harvester felt their market share plunge as cheaper imports entered the country. In the 1980s, America felt the sting of a serious recession. Battles were waged between unions and companies reeling from the need for modernization and the loss of competitive position in world markets. Cooperation between union and management turned into bitter wrangling.

At such conflicts, Liberals and Socialists jump in and drumbeat loudly for more government control of key industries, while lamenting over the "plight of the worker." Pretty soon the general population is swayed into believing that only government is capable of running big business. But, if the government owned key industries, the unions would become their "enforcers" of policy in business. Is this not socialism where the workers do the bidding of their task masters to meet government wage and output objectives? Isn't this the same failed system that saps worker initiative and industry innovation? And when this industry of overpaid workers, antiquated equipment, and underproduction can't compete in the world market, will a government subsidy paid from tax revenues be the ready answer? Soon the products of such a business would be too expensive to compete in the world market, so such a government could solve that problem by prohibiting competitive imports. Suddenly, that hefty paycheck bargained for "you" by a self-serving union is being eaten to pieces by high taxes and pricey goods. What now the "plight of the worker?"

Therefore, American Laborer, while there's still a chance, ask yourself why the Democratic Party is so closely allied with unions. Think more independently of your union's position on politics; is the union serving its own ends or yours and the company's together? Take a serious look at what the business you work for has to offer, not only to you, but also to your customers, your country's economy, and the innovations that improve efficiency, industry prosperity, and job security in the long-run.

II. Socialism and Society

Chapter 5
Dependency:
Keeping Minorities in Chains

In feudal days, the castle dwellers kept the serfs dependent on them through class suppression and the promise of protection in times of attack. In the 18th century, the royals of Europe kept the servant classes overworked and tied to their masters through an over-emphasized cultural obligation. During the slave years, plantation owners kept their slaves subdued with forced labor and by prohibiting their education. Even after slavery was outlawed in America, black citizens were continually suppressed and discriminated against, making it almost impossible for them to rise out of poverty. Finally, because of the civil rights movement, education, opportunity, and improved social attitudes; there is enough of everything for those who can work for it.

Over the last several decades, our government developed assistance programs to help the poor–particularly poor blacks and other poor minority groups–to make it through rough times. Although originally established for good reasons, time has shown that too often these programs keep their beneficiaries stuck at a subsistence level of existence. How could this happen?

Primarily, by making government-controlled programs readily available, no effort was required on the part of the beneficiary of that program to earn his or her "pay." In essence, the beneficiary's "job" became meeting requirements of the program in order to collect a check. (Anyone who has ever collected unemployment benefits understands this. Simply meet the requirements of *looking* for a job, and the check comes. The difference between unemployment benefits and say, Medicaid, however, is that unemployment benefits are temporary.) Meanwhile, the poor get poorer, not necessarily because the rich get richer, but because those poor who rely on the government for their subsistence never enjoy the benefits and satisfaction of earning and learning a living. They are dead-ended into a lack of self assurance and self worth, leading to self doubt, to the point where they think that only the government can provide for their needs.

But it isn't the government so much as the working segment of the population who pays the taxes from which entitlement programs are paid. The result is two segments of society: one that relies on the government for support, and another that works feverishly to support itself *and* the tax burden. In nearly every case, it's the Democratic Party that promotes tax increases on the working segment of the population while offering more entitlement programs to the poor. In this way, Democrats buy votes from the disenfranchised, while keeping them at a subsistence level of existence. In essence, they are crippling minorities for the party's own gain.

This strategy of seducing the discontented by giving them something for nothing has been used by developing communist nations of the past and present. But there is a price: dependency. Black Americans in particular, whose ancestors rose out of slavery, fought discrimination in the Jim Crow years, and finally achieved equality in education and society, are being rechained by the very programs originally designed to help them. And it's not just poor blacks, but newer immigrants to this country as well–all being courted by the promise of a free ride and fashioned into pawns of socialism.

Don't let this happen to you. Don't settle for subsistence living as offered by government handouts. Instead, support those who curb taxes and encourage the kind of free enterprise that makes jobs and breaks the bondage of dependency.

Chapter 6
An Unbiased Media?

Today's newspapers complain that they are losing subscribers, advertisers, and money. They say that computers, the Internet, and television are cutting into their readership. Although these factors play a part, there is another significant reason for their decline: readers are fed up with the biased slant between the pages.

Most journalists would bristle at the thought that they could be biased. After all, the noble intent of the profession is to report the unvarnished truth, like it or not; to provide balanced coverage of both sides of an issue without showing partiality. Weakening this lofty goal, however, are several human factors. First, the personality type most attracted to journalism and entertainment belongs to people who shirk convention. Their thirst to question why things are is a valuable trait to offer society, but when it turns into an outright dismissal of *all* established ideas, that type of journalism is biased.

Another threat to unbiased reporting comes from journalism academies. A certain amount of indoctrination and political slant attaches itself to any major in college, and journalism is no exception. But the other career's graduates aren't writing newspapers and anchoring TV broadcasts. If a reporter's opinions or politics–or those of their employers–slant the news, millions of people are misled.

A third influence worth mentioning here is how newspapers across the country rely on syndicated columns from *The New York Times* and *Los Angeles Times*; both known liberal-leaning publications. *The New York Times* recently took a hit to its credibility when it fabricated a story [note that this wasn't its first offense]. In such cases, "Don't believe everything you read," takes on the ominous new meaning: "Who else is making things up?" How do we discern between an honest mistake and intent, when a front page error on Sunday shows up as back page correction on Monday? And finally, when "the funnies" are no longer just comic relief, but pushing political propaganda–at our children, no less–one can see why newspapers are losing readership across the country.

As a primarily liberal establishment, the press must beware that it doesn't take that next step left and become a pawn of a socialist agenda. The socialist philosophy "the end justifies the means" translates into a manipulation of the facts to benefit one party over another and reinforce the tenets of the socialist point of view. Slanting the news to push politics is not unbiased reporting. Under such conditions, the public cannot read the news with the confidence that even an attempt was made at fair reporting.

While the press might at least struggle to give a less biased report, the entertainment industry doesn't have to try at all. As mentioned earlier in this chapter, performance careers tend to attract people who resist convention and authority. These folks also value experimentation and impulse, all useful talents and viewpoints when you're an actor honing your craft. But these same characteristics are destructive when applied to the entire population. Read on for an explanation . . .

When movies and television were new, the cultural mores of the larger body of society influenced the content. For example, an actress might have played a chaste woman on the big screen, even though in her real life she was having multiple affairs. Or an actor may have played a stalwart hero, but in his real life was battling alcoholism. TV families were portrayed as happy and functional, while the "real" families at home looked on in their imperfection. This situation created a perceived hypocrisy that rankled the "free-thinking" natures of those in the entertainment industry.

As time passed, the writers and performers injected more and more of their own perspectives and politics into television and movies. Some for the good, but others much to the detriment of mankind. They rejected the old illusion that every family was functional, and replaced it with a new, just as false concept that every family is *dis*functional. By broadcasting these ideas, the industry gave the illusion that "everyone is like this," when in fact, it was a handful of the population telling the rest what to think and how to be; a small, careless segment of the population, raising generations of TV and movie viewers in its own image. Instead of giving their viewers something to aspire to, they gave them something to live down to. All the while weaving a pro-left, anti-right, political theme throughout. Paving the way for socialist intrusion.

Although a few skilled and brilliant politicians began their careers as actors, the vast majority of performers are just that: performers, not political science majors. And yet, it is a common occurrence to see famous actors impart their minuscule grasp of the issues as authoritative fact, whether or not they are accurate, tested, or true. And they do so through a national–and even global–forum, effectively distorting reality and bending society to erred conclusions.

Ironically, by pushing loose ethics and leftist thinking the entertainment industry is forming its own demise. History has shown that when society gets too decadent, oppressive government comes in to restore order. After all, Hollywood is big business, and socialism is bad for business. Entertainment invites "thinking out of the box" and socialism would write all the plots and censor unauthorized ideas. Artistic personality types tend to resist structure and control, and socialism is all about controlling every aspect of life.

By letting liberal concepts dominate the news and entertainment worlds, journalists and performers alike are jeopardizing the very thing most dear to their hearts: the right to free speech and freedom of the press in America.

Chapter 7
National Medical Insurance: Would This "Cure" Be Worse Than the Disease?

The United States has among the best medical facilities, medications, talent, and equipment in the world. But medical costs, insurance rates, and prescription drug prices are out of hand. The problem has spawned a great debate in this country over how to provide adequate medical care for all citizens on an equitable basis. Before we assume that a national government-run insurance plan is the only solution, however, let's look at the interrelating factors that have created this escalation in medical costs.

The first factor is spending attitudes. Over the last several decades, Americans have come to expect that little or no money for medical services must come out of their own pockets. They now believe that if they are going to pay premiums, then the insurance companies should require minimal deductions yet cover all medical costs. Note that these are often the same people willing to buy cars and boats with borrowed money, save up for vacations, buy expensive game systems for their kids, and spend vast sums on restaurant food, beverages, and tobacco. They get so caught up in consumerism that they resent spending money on their own medical coverage.

To attract this new brand of customer, insurance companies have lowered their deductibles and offered creative coverage packages. They've done this in order to maintain the cash flow that funds their reserves and investments while also paying out claims. Their customers, meanwhile, in an effort to make the most of their premiums, are running to the doctor for minor ailments like never before, whereas a "wait and see" position would have shown most of these minor ailment cases being adequately handled in the home.

Another factor pushing up medical costs is prescription drug marketing. Every day the drug companies inundate print and broadcast media with ads that say "ask your doctor..." about the latest drug for an ever-increasing list of maladies. Now doctors get the drug company sales pitch from the drug reps *and* their patients. More and more demand from the public for doctors to prescribe drug treatment leads to the inevitable economics maxim of the seller charging what the market will bear. This over-prescribing of drugs has driven up prices and led to the well-documented offshoot problems of increased drug dependencies and antibiotic-resistant strains of bacteria.

As the overwhelming demand for services contributes to the rise in medical costs, insurance companies raise their rates to keep up. In fact, these rates have risen so fast that a bigger and bigger segment of the public can no longer afford any coverage, and businesses are hard put to offer medical coverage as a benefit. The lower middle class, not wealthy enough to afford insurance, and not poor enough to qualify for Medicaid, is the hardest hit. Medical disasters have financially wiped out individuals and their families. The problem is real and Liberals are touting a national medical insurance as the solution. Even doctors, long against such a program, are starting to consider it in the recognition that something must change.

But inviting socialized medicine into the equation would be like planting kudzu in the Carolinas to battle soil erosion. Soon government involvement would strangle the whole process. Here's how: under a national medical insurance program, individual, professional, and financial incentives for medical providers would fade away. Government employees would decide who was sick enough for care, what care they should receive, how much it would cost, and how much the providers would be compensated. If too many people are running to the doctor for minor ailments now, imagine how often they'd go if they thought they didn't have to pay for it at all! But that's the irony. They *would* be paying for it; through a national insurance premium *and* higher taxes issued to cover the extra expense of an over-used service.

No, nationalizing medical insurance and opening another window to socialism is not the answer. Instead, by letting patients, drug companies, and providers (doctors, technicians, etc.) remain individually responsible and motivated to play their parts in the medical system, the best interests of all are served. So under this scenario, how can Americans keep down costs and make medical care readily available to all citizens?

The answer is neither a "quick fix" (like the drug companies claim when advertising their products), nor an "easy answer" (as the Liberals unrealistically promise in their campaign speeches), but it is a *real* solution that would drop costs and make services more available to all. The answer is a combined effort between the private sector, government pressure, and a change in American attitudes.

Public attitude triggered the current healthcare mess, and public attitudes will reverse it. Smart Americans who reprioritize healthcare to the top of their list, will realize that if they can afford a $200 game system, they can afford a $200 doctor visit. The middle income individual, instead of running to the doctor to justify his premium under a low-deductible policy, will now, reevaluate his own or his children's illness and determine if it is truly worth a doctor visit. Why? Because his financial commitment is involved.

The reduced demand for doctor visits means doctors may apply their services to more meaningful care. Stacks of paperwork for unnecessary claims and frivolous visits would shrink, thereby saving doctors, staff, and insurance companies huge amounts of time and money. (Compare this savings to the expense of a bureaucracy required to support a national insurance program!) As the demand for minor services goes down, medical and insurance rates would fall as well.

As for the times this Smart American must fork over the cash for treatment, he'll know that he is still paying less under the new plan than the old. Here's how: Families who pay $12,000 a year for medical insurance have typically an actual medical cost of $2,500 per year that the insurance company pays under a low-deductible plan. That's a lot of fun money left over for the family that elects to self-insure its typical and routine medical problems. They'd save money by using their high deductible/low premium policy to protect them in the unlikelier event of a serious accident or illness. Even a $10,000 deductible that someone *might* have to pay in the event of a high-cost medical incident, is still less than the $12,000 they *will* be paying, year after year, for low-deductible insurance, claims or no claims.

What about the poor folks to whom a $10,000 deductible, for example, would be a crushing amount? That's where the government comes in. State senators and governors could influence insurance companies and financial institutions to develop programs that establish deductible rates for the poor; and urge credit card companies to provide a low permanently fixed interest rate credit card, regardless of credit history, for medical purchases only. This card would enable anyone (not just the very poor) to obtain prescriptions and medical care when the need arose, whether or not one could afford it at the time. So, just as a person pays off a planned debt (i.e., for a car or braces) over time, they can pay off an unplanned medical bill (broken arm treatment, for example), but at a more forgiving rate. As part of the negotiations, plans could be drawn up for those debtors who fall into further poverty and need Medicaid's help to pay the bill.

Government representatives can also negotiate to eliminate pre-existing condition restrictions while also helping insurance companies form plans to spread risk. They can ease the tax burden on private business which, in tandem with the falling medical insurance rates, would enable more companies to offer insurance benefits again. Our elected officials must push for reductions in malpractice lawsuit awards to better reflect actual damages. They must also aggressively address fraudulent claims. These include the groundless "blackmail letters" (i.e., "settle out of court or we will sue") from lawyers to doctors for the purpose of profiting from these pay-outs.

These joint efforts would reduce doctors' malpractice insurance burdens and fraudulent malpractice threats; and the cost of medical care falls even more.

This multi-step response to the medical care issue means that over their lifetimes, people will pay less for medical insurance than they do now, and less for their medical services, *even if* they should max out their high deductibles. The cost of those services would come down while making care available to all. A whole new capability for servicing the needs of the elderly and indigent would now be realized.

Under the current costly system, the poor person who can't afford insurance often waits too long to see a doctor, and when he finally goes, the illness has progressed to an advanced state, both more life threatening and more expensive. The burden is greater on the individual's health, his wallet, or on the agency that pays the bill when the patient can't. Under the new proposal, lower medical and insurance rates would mean more people could afford to fund their own medical care. And for those people who couldn't, the low-rate, medical-specific credit cards would help them get the care when they needed it. Both rich and poor will take on a more purposeful attitude toward their family's health–choosing their own doctors and shopping around for services–and pay for preventive care with their own monetary sources as good and valid expenditures. And they'll have the additional security of knowing they are covered in the event of catastrophic events.

Additionally, since demand for doctor visits will be thus reduced, doctors and nurses may apply their services to more meaningful care. And staffing shortages for caregivers will be a thing of the past due to the reductions in costs, paperwork and busy work now used to fund administrative personnel requirements. An added benefit would be that caregivers would have an increase in job reward and satisfaction.

Just as a low-deductible insurance policy has no real savings to offer, a nationalized medical insurance program is no real solution at all. Let's not vote in a policy where the cure is worse than the disease. A basic attitude change by the citizens of this country will preserve the enormous strengths of our private medical system, and make its services more accessible and affordable to all.

Chapter 8
Nature: Pawn or Plunder?

Watch television and you'll see hurricanes, tsunamis, droughts and floods. According to the documentaries and dramas, the world is coming to an end, these disasters are humanity's fault, and because people won't change, only government can fix it. A large segment of society believes this, but should they? Let's look at these claims one by one.

It's humanity's fault. Humans have polluted the air and waters, damaged ecosystems, and caused extinction of many species; it's true. But can we really take *all* the blame for global warming? Can our influences really be greater than the effects of the sun, sun spot activity, and minute changes in the earth's orbit? What about the effects of the earth wobbling on its axis, changing the position of the poles over decades, centuries and millennia? Our actions have contributed to our surroundings, and we certainly must be responsible stewards of the earth and its resources. However, let's not overstate our impact on global warming. Non-human causes of climate change are far beyond our ability to control. We should not become so preoccupied with a one-degree climate difference that we overlook more clear-cut dangers to man and his environment, such as, for example, a rogue nation's fanatical leaders and their pursuit of nuclear weapons for power advancement.

People won't change. A mix of public pressure and laws has done some wacky things at times, but at other times has cleaned up rivers, improved air quality, preserved wildernesses, and so on. While the environmental issue has been used as a scare tactic by Liberals to push for more government control, the concern remains that left to their own devices, many people would carry on as they always have, consuming what they wish, profiting from natural resources, and leave it up to everyone else to "do the right thing."

Interestingly enough, however, more and more people *are* doing "the right thing." They are recycling, and making and buying more environmentally friendly products. In their best American ingenuity fashion, businesses are finding ways to make "green" profitable. There is more to be done, but the trend is underway. And it's possible because our structure of democracy and free enterprise encourages prosperity. Freedom and prosperity breed hope, and hope makes people responsible because they believe that their actions can make a difference. For a litmus test, compare the streets of a slum to those of a middle-class neighborhood. It's not the street-cleaners or the laws that keeps those suburb streets clean. It's every resident picking up after himself, and together effecting a positive change.

Only government can fix it. If that were true, then communist China's burgeoning economy wouldn't be soiling the air and waters the way it currently is. Yet socialist-leaning democrats in this country would have you believe that only a strong central government can save the environment. They are using the global warming issue to extend their influence over other nations. But by ostensibly getting nations to unite over the attack on greenhouse gases, they risk weakening free industrial nations. Here's how it's done: by enacting sweeping environmental laws over industrialized nations, those industries would be forced to change methods, thereby slowing output and increasing cost of products. Countries not so burdened by the enforcement could easily undercut prices to compete. Participating and nonparticipating countries who would likely ignore the environmental controls could use their cheap labor or socialist-state provided subsidies to cheapen their prices. As one of the largest industrial nations in the world, the United States would be a big loser. A better strategy would be to share new, cleaner technologies and let up-and-coming nations learn from, not repeat, the mistakes of America and other enterprising countries. Let's not "punish" America and her contemporary countries through drastic after-the-fact environmental sanctions.

Nature as our model. Scientists stress the interconnectedness of all species and natural phenomenon on earth. It is this very relationship that demands that we humans take every step with care. That includes actions designed to preserve our natural resources. If we enacted environmental laws too sudden, stifling, and severe for businesses to bear, we'd cause widespread industry closures, unemployment, and drops in income. Countries that rely on American markets and spending would find their economies affected as well. At the extreme, unrest could lead to war. And war means the use of devastating weapons that decimate humans and countryside alike.

Our concern for the environment must factor in all the ramifications of each proposed "green law" so we don't do more harm than good. Consider the interconnectedness of these examples: Glass containers are more recyclable then plastic, but their production consumes far more energy. Glass is also heavier, upping trip counts and fuel consumption. Decades of forest fire suppression has built up understory growth, thereby fueling more ecologically devastating fires. Soy-based inks are kinder to the environment, but soy fields are among the crops replacing rain forests in South America. Plant-based ethanol is an alternative fuel to gasoline, but will lead to wheat shortages in Europe and corn shortages in the U.S. due to transfer of those foods to ethanol production. If ethanol demand increases, will more forests be leveled to make room for fuel crops? Oil drilling has been restricted for fear of spillage accidents, yet more spill damage has been caused by oil tankers that still travel the world's oceans than by any pipeline break or on-site pumping rig accident.

True, if you let only businessmen make the decisions, they would do what's profitable and put the environment at risk. Likewise, if you let only environmentalists make the decisions, they would jeopardize economics and cause widespread unrest and harm. That is why our current checks and balance system is the best way to address these environmental issues.

Just as nature always finds equilibrium in the tug-of-war between the species, so too has our nation enjoyed relative stability through the checks and balances set forth by our founding fathers when they formed our democracy. Their foresight has helped to curb power excesses by either branch, prevented many a whim from being made into law, and safeguarded against one interest taking precedence over all others. Through this process many laws already exist to prevent environmental damage, and to clean up "dirty" industries. Our weakness has been in enforcement–and particularly *equal* enforcement–of these laws. Big as well as small businesses should be made to comply. But the government's involvement must remain limited to oversight and enforcement. The laws themselves come from the people. Balance is achieved through compromise between disparate interests. Through due process of law, measured changes give businesses time to adapt and recover. Under these guidelines, we'll continue to improve our ability to protect the environment and our economy at the same time.

III. Socialism and the Family

Chapter 9
So, Who Needs Marriage?

Picture early man, scrounging and scavenging about, seizing food and mating opportunities where he could. Imagine the children of those parents, children of the same mother, but different fathers; no certainty, no security, little more than intelligent animals, but barely aware of themselves, much less each other. Enter marriage. A dedicated union between man and woman in accordance with natural law, cementing affection and cooperation between two individuals, finding fulfillment through love and understanding. Love, security, and responsibility passed on to their offspring and to society as a whole. A mere pack of homo sapiens becomes a village of people. No longer like animals, but evolved, spiritual beings. It's no wonder that mankind came to understand that marriage is instituted by God.

Over time, even governments recognized the stabilizing effects of marriage on society.

Marriage became not only a religious ceremony, but a civil contract as well. Civil structures encouraged marriage as a permanent union, but also provided the means of determining property and rights issues for the times marriages came apart. The value of the traditional family unit can be found in its predominance of success stories versus failures. Conversely, where this unit has been fractured by fad (i.e., pop culture) or abuse (such as the taking of pre-pubescent wives in some tribal cultures) or historical atrocities (slavery and war), emotional, financial, and ethical hardships abound.

Socialism, nevertheless, looks at marriage as an artificial and unnecessary union between man and woman. In socialism's view, marriage interferes with social planning. It complicates the ability to control society. It weakens socialism's attempt to push parents aside and indoctrinate a nation's children to its own ideals. (If you don't think this is possible, remember Hitler's Youth, communist indoctrination, al-Queda terrorist cells, and Wahabiism).

Consciously or not, American Liberals are pushing a socialist agenda by undermining traditional marriage and the family unit. They have taken the valid women's rights issue and altered it to suggest that a woman who foregoes a career to stay home and raise her children is somehow demeaning herself. In the name of planned parenthood, they chastise women who have more children than what social planners advise to make up a family of the "right size." They shout "women's rights" to justify abortion and claim "progressive thinking" when promoting state-run childcare.

But once you remove the necessity and the sanctity of marriage from mankind, you remove the core essential of what is most needed between all people (unselfish love) and you dismantle the primary care for their offspring so essential to forming a new generation. Confident, caring, productive children of a happy, stable family environment don't need a government to step in on their behalf. They need a government that values marriage, so more kids can grow up surrounded by security and love.

Chapter 10
A Proof for Human Life

Consider the mother of a two-year-old child. Suppose, she is too young to be a mother or too poor to support the child; perhaps unwed, or physically or emotionally unfit for the responsibility; doesn't want to add to the population problem; or simply doesn't want to be a mother just yet, or ever. Suppose she doesn't want to turn over the child to adoption and live with the perceived stigma of having failed the child in some way, or that the child may return to her life later and complicate it. After much anguish, she decides that because the child is her child, and the product of her body, she will decide on the best solution. So, with the help of her doctor, she ends the child's life. A jury would have little difficulty sending that woman and her doctor to jail for murder.

Now suppose all the same reasons existed for taking that child's life, but it was six months old, or six days old, or six seconds old. The jury's decision would still be the same. Rewind time a little further to a child still inside the womb, and suddenly the verdict varies by month of pregnancy and state of residence: was it lawful abortion or murder? Clearly, therefore, the crux of this controversial issue lies not in the *reasons* for abortion, but in the *definition of human life*. When does life begin?

For an explanation of what it means to be called human, let's look at science. Mankind has discovered an order in nature so profound that it has provided us with the ability to define all living things by a molecule called DNA. With DNA we can clearly differentiate between genus and species, plant and animal, and between individuals. All living individuals have a unique DNA code. Therefore, by this code, humans can be defined in matter as distinct from all other matter, and as individuals, one person different from all others.

Science has also revealed that only human cells have 46 chromosomes, distinguishing them from all other living creatures. Even a woman and man's reproductive cells, the egg and sperm, are not complete life forms as such, but haploid (containing only half the chromosomes necessary to produce a cell complete for the creation of life). Once the egg is fertilized, the cell becomes diploid (containing all the chromosomes necessary for life) and is therefore considered a *life form*. This cell (called zygote, from the Greek word *zygotes*, meaning united) has the recognizable DNA coding for an individual human being. A *life*– defined by any dictionary as an organized body that grows and develops, as this human cell does, but not into an organ, or bone, or other life-sustaining part of the mother's body, but into a unique, complete individual.

It is important to recognize the distinction that this unborn child is *in* the mother, and *dependent on* the mother, but is not *of* the mother. This child has all the coded essentials in its makeup for a complete and separate human being. It needs only the protection and nurturing by its mother's body during pregnancy, and by its family after birth to develop into a complete adult.

Now, because this unborn child is *in* the mother and not *of* the mother, it is entitled to the same protections of all people. The respect for human dignity demands it. Further, a child conceived in the U.S. is entitled to the same unalienable rights of life, liberty and the pursuit of happiness as any other American child. To deny these rights discriminates against the unborn in the favor of the born. No person has the right to subjugate those rights. Not the state, not the parents, nor society as a whole.

Yet Socialists, Liberals, and the Democratic Party–for the sake of convenience, expedience, and social planning–have succeeded in creating a law that ends human life. They presume that mankind can take upon itself the determining power of what is human life and what is not. This presumption is of such magnitude that it goes beyond all that was intended for the existence of man. This grievous action, if left unchecked, will bear consequences not yet imagined. After all, who else is inconvenient, not wanted, expensive, or in the way? Barbarous regimes of the past and present have labeled entire peoples as disposable and murdered millions.

By promoting abortion as a solution, we commit a crime against humanity just as awful as the ancients who stoned any woman found pregnant out of wedlock. Conversely, a vote for respecting life is a vote to protect and nurture the rights of *all* humans: born or unborn, married or single, man or woman, child or adult, helpless or strong; regardless of race, religion, and heritage. Now *that's* American. Not only is it American, it preserves the sanctity of human life.

Chapter 11
A Legal *and* Moral Case
for Respecting Life

Roe vs. Wade is already invalid. Why? Because the Supreme Court admitted in its 1973 decision that no such "right" to an abortion would exist if Congress were to establish unborn children as "persons." Well, the legal proof of the unborn's "personhood" is being proven every day.

Doctors are operating on babies still in the womb. Premature birth survivals are happening earlier and earlier in pregnancies. DNA science is being applied, not only to prove human evidence in crimes, but as a means of identifying one's human offspring in custody and child support cases. Pregnant women involved in attacks or accidents have successfully sued for manslaughter when their unborn son or daughter died as a result of these events. By science and legal precedence, the proof of the unborn person already exists. With evidence like this, why aren't pro-life advocates hiring an army of lawyers to overturn *Roe vs. Wade?* There are two predominant reasons:

The first complication to reversing *Roe vs. Wade* is what to call the abortions that occur after the law changes. Would they be redefined as murder, and if so, the people involved, murderers? Some fear that this scenario would cause a return of dangerous "back-street" abortions. But consider the changing times. Pregnant unmarried woman are not ostracized like they once were. Nor are illegitimate children. Childless parents are going overseas to adopt children because of the shortage of adoptable babies in America. Many key arguments that lead to the *Roe vs. Wade* result have expired.

In the wake of an overthrow of the *Roe vs. Wade* decision, a possible strategy could be a period of amnesty when the anti-abortion law is suspended while our country cultivates a "culture of embracing new life." More networks would be set up between families wishing to adopt, and pregnant girls and women who carry a child needing adoption. Schools and religious education programs should continue emphasizing abstinence, waiting, consequences of pregnancy, pregnancy prevention, and self-respect issues. In science and/or health classes, "life in the womb" photos and documentaries can be presented to fully educate teens about human development. Communities could revamp old chaperonage customs to match modern times. Media and ad council groups could set standards to eliminate overtly sexual ads. Even entertainment and fine art entities could hold round-table discussions to discourage art for the sake of sexual promiscuity, and promiscuity for the sake of art.

Meanwhile, Congress would be drafting new "unborn child" laws for when the amnesty period is over. These would include defining the various stages of pregnancy, and mothers' mental and environment conditions as they would apply to abortion penalties. For example, a 30-year-old woman who has an abortion to hide an affair would be judged differently from a 14-year-old girl who sought an abortion to avoid the wrath of an abusive father. Because of the emotional complexities of pregnancy and abortion, and the immaturity of young teens, compassion and counseling must be part of the remedy.

There is another reason *Roe vs. Wade* is not being overthrown, despite mounting legal and scientific evidence for "personhood" before birth. Liberal elements in politics and the media, in concert with socialist thinking, are stonewalling the change. Socialist philosophy does not allow for moral law; only civil law. As any first-year law student will tell you, "It's neither right or wrong; it's just the law." To the socialist, it is important to instill in the minds of the general population that abortion is good for society and that the individual, not moral law, should determine if abortion should be allowed. Socialism requires that all aspects of society be controlled by a central government, from economic output to consumption of goods. Therefore, when goods and services are considered at capacity, then consumption can be controlled through reducing the population. Once socialist strategies have rendered abortion socially acceptable, then the government can make abortion *mandatory* whenever circumstances recommend it. The social planners would have unconscionable power, should they hold in their hands the keys to our existence.

Since the *Roe vs. Wade* decision in 1973, well over 48 million would-be Americans have been aborted. That number is greater than all the war-related American deaths that occurred during the last century.* Our country's customs and traditions have always emphasized the rights of all individuals. Through a sometimes tortuous, but always upward climb to moral enlightenment, these rights have been extended to former slaves, women, native tribes, and immigrants. Before the *Roe vs. Wade* decision, even unborn babies had as much a right to live as the mothers who carried them. *It's only recently that the liberals and socialist-leaning Democrats have adopted a culture of death over a culture of life. They've duped the gullible of this country into believing one of the greatest travesties in American history: that the elimination of*

millions of unborn innocents is socially
responsible.

It's time to act! Don't let the liberals'
"ends justify the means" brand of twisted logic
divert you from the truth: the beating heart of
the unborn child is the same beating heart after
the child leaves the womb. Conception is the
only clear delineation between non-person and
human being. Pregnancy might be an
inconvenience for some, but in itself it is *not*
evil. Babies are good. Life is good. The
sanctity of life is worth protecting!

*Statistics of Note

American combat deaths:
W.W.I - 53,402
W.W.II - 292,000
Korean War - 33,700
Vietnam War - 47,359
Desert Storm - 148
Iraqi War - 3900 (this number includes hostile and
non-hostile causes of death)
Total in the last century = 430,509

American abortions in the 34 years since Roe vs.
Wade - 48,000,000. That's 111 times all the American
combat deaths in the last 100 years.

Estimated illegal aliens working and living in the
United States - 16-20 million.

Approximate number of aborted Americans that would
be working age today - 20 million.

IV. Socialism and Philosophy

Chapter 12
Theocracies: "Believe Our Way or Die"

A beautiful testament to the American way of life has been the appreciation of faith in our society. The establishment of freedom of religion and the deliberate separation of an organized religion from dominion over our society, has allowed every citizen free devotion to their particular faith. How is it, then, that liberals who discredit religion in America at every turn, are the same people who support a "live and let live" policy with theocracies that persecute and massacre their citizens who don't practice the church of the state? The answer to this riddle lies, ironically, in the similarities between socialist and theocratic creeds.

Terrorist movements form when extremist cults branch off from their original benevolent and peaceful faith roots. These sects distort their original creeds into self-serving theocracies to center government power in the clergy. Promising their believers eternal paradise in the next life, the leaders manipulate the population into committing *un*godly atrocities to further state agendas. Like socialism, the theocracy eliminates human rights for all citizens except those that follow its strict creed. In socialism, the state is the preemptive power; in a theocracy, the clergy become the state. Both regimes believe the ends justify the means.

What a travesty to use the word "religion" to describe a philosophy that promotes murder, torture, and suicide to achieve its goals. Heinous crimes are not principles of faith. They are diametrically opposed to a true faith's understanding of the sanctity of human life, and peace and good will to be enjoyed by all mankind.

Nevertheless, American Liberals and their politicians think that fanatical theocracies have a right to succeed. They believe our country should not interfere when so many innocent lives are being persecuted and murdered by these regimes. Liberal thinkers say the United States aggravated terrorist countries into a hate position. In reality, theocracies were built on a hate that thrives even without outside encouragement, and without intent to change. Theocratic fanatics will attempt to destroy what America stands for, and with whatever weapons they have at their disposal.

At the time of this writing, about 3,900 precious American lives have been lost in the fight to free Iraqi citizens from a brutal regime and to protect our nation from its terrorist threat. Liberal politicians are reluctant to acknowledge the successes of this campaign and instead are urging for a recall of troops. They cite casualty counts and objective delays to support their point. But what do they really care about? Aren't these the same politicians whose support of legalized abortion has meant the taking of millions of unborn human lives? Why are these same politicians seemingly less concerned over the hundreds of thousands murdered by Saddam Hussein's former regime? From whence, then, do the liberals' sudden compassion for human life spring?

In reality, the "pull out now" advocates are *extending* the fight by making the terrorists think they are winning. It emboldens them to continue their terrorist actions. But by staying in Iraq and crippling al-Queda and terrorist perpetrators, we keep the terrorists too preoccupied to reorganize, thus reducing their strikes against their own people and other nations. Until the job is done and a free Iraq is on the way to a successful democracy, American leaders should support our troops there, not sabotage their efforts with selfish political agendas. To mislabel the effort a "failed war" so that the Democrats might win the next election, is to dishonor every American that died for this cause; is to endanger the soldiers still fighting the fight; is to feed the terrorists' lust for mayhem. Careless rhetoric empowers fanatic regimes–like Iran and other countries dominated by religious terrorists–to continue their violent horrors in the Middle East and around the world.

Americans, use your votes wisely! Be sure your votes are securing our country's freedoms, and *not* encouraging the dangerous and unstable central power of a theocracy.

Chapter 13
The Veiled Conceit of Humanism

America's founding politicians were men of faith. They applied many of their religious principles to the formation of our country's government (equality, justice, blessings of liberty, etc.). Despite their religious convictions, they wanted to be sure that all citizens could worship freely and that no one faith would dominate through the power of government. Not Protestantism, not Catholicism, not Judaism, nor even Shintoism. Odd then, that another "ism" has woven its way into the fabric of today's American government. That philosophy is humanism.

Humanism attempts to elevate mankind to a supreme level. That is, that man, through his evolution, is capable of being a self-determiner of what is good. To a Humanist, there is no such thing as evil, only the absence of good. What is good will be determined by people. After all, humanism has as its basic premise that people are rational beings who possess within themselves the capacity for truth and goodness.

But this premise is in conflict with man's concupiscence, that is, our animal nature. Because of this earthiness, we are not capable of being sole determiner of what is good or evil. Our physical senses and appetites tend us towards basic survival instincts. Humanists believe that the religious principles that bring order and conscience are archaic in the new world and no longer necessary. How wrong they are! Without spiritual guidance, our baser instincts would take over defining what's good and evil to suit selfish interest. As these interests pulled at the law and order established for our country, anarchy would result.

Liberals resist traditional definitions of good and evil. Humanism allows Liberals to rewrite ethics and shout "matter of interpretation" when challenged. When humanism goes unchecked and breaks down the order of a society, socialism steps into the breach. Then socialism can apply humanism to its own ends. No longer will religion or spiritual values have any meaning. Social planners will define what's right and wrong.

Wouldn't you rather a country be a diverse body of conscientious, faith-inspired citizens? In America, that's what we are. Let's keep it that way.

Chapter 14
One Nation, Built on Faith

"Congress shall make no law respecting an establishment of religion, or prohibiting the free exercise thereof;..." so begins the Bill of Rights to the Constitution of the United States.

This precept took first position in the Bill of Rights because of the importance of religion in our founders' lives. Many of them and their forebears came here from Europe to escape religious persecution and to freely practice their faith. While no church was to be incorporated within our government, the writers of the Declaration of Independence and our Constitution applied sound religious and philosophical principles to its formation; even referencing God and the Creator in their writings.

This precept has since been referred to as "separation of church and state." It was not phrased "separation of *God* and state" because our founders clearly wanted their Creator's blessings over the new nation. By separating the state from any formal church organization, they promoted free worship for all its citizens. Faith was so woven through the fabric of each day that prayer at public forums and functions was commonplace.

Today, "separation of church and state" is being touted by liberals as a legal justification to prohibit prayer in schools and other public places. But they are changing the original intention of the Bill of Rights. Public prayer has nothing to do with the "church and state" issue. It is merely a bond of spirit; an invitation for participation in the invocation of one's God in reverence, thanksgiving or request for help. And when one has *no* god, they are free to *not* believe and *not* pray, without fear of legal retribution, thanks to the efforts of our nation's predominantly Christian founders.

Regarding prayer in public places, those liberals and agnostics who fear brain-washing, judgmentalism, or merely resist tradition, would do well to remember that our deeply religious forefathers could have crafted a theocracy for their new government, but didn't. Instead, since our nation's birth, many immigrants have fled to our shores to escape theocracies (where one church is the law) and godless communisms (where no church is the law). Socialism, in fact, has never been supportive of religion. Those concepts are in conflict with socialism's requirement that you be dependent on the state, not upon yourself or your God.

But separation of church and state has been good for the American government and for its citizens' diverse religions. It has guaranteed that churches and government be watchdogs for each other. Laws penalize misrepresentation and fraud by faux or corrupted churches. People of faith can demand ethical standards from their political representatives. Or is that what the liberal politicians are really afraid of: scrutiny by a faith-based citizenry? That's why we must not support the "separation of *God* and state" philosophy put out by liberal politicians. In the United States of America, our *strength* comes from our beliefs in a Creator. To abandon ourselves to a godless national political system could only mean the degradation of our American way of life. When men and women of faith participate in government, and vote responsibly, our freedoms are preserved.

So pray out loud in public if you want to. Thanks to our Constitution, just as no law can force you to do it, no law may forbid it either.

Conclusion

To some, the title "Socialism: A growing malignancy in America" sounds like melodramatic exaggeration. But in truth, the words describe a real threat to the American way of life.

Just as a malignant tumor spreads its malignancy through a human body while the person is still well, so too, are liberal philosophies being spread through our socioeconomic structure while our freedoms are still intact. Liberal elements in politics, the media, and entertainment are blasting or belittling traditional values while presuming to speak for the rest of us. More educators are injecting humanism into their curriculum, sometimes even in the early grades. As for college, that setting has always been a fertile ground for liberal views. There arrive the young adults, ready to test their new freedom, but reluctant to take on the responsibilities of full adulthood. In this mindset they are easily wooed by the liberal premise that "nothing is bad, do whatever you want, and let the government do all the hard stuff for you." In the past, most students survived this temporary wayward period in their lives, but now, they are showing up for college pre-primed by the media to accept this rubbish. As a result, jaded teachings are destroying or distorting traditional and valuable lessons associated with American history and the higher callings of mankind.

Regarding the challenges of environmental threats, accessible medical care, and poverty relief, Americans are among the most proactive and charitable in the world. Yet Liberals wave these topics like storm warning flags; leveraging emotion and fear to attain their goals. Conservative Democrats and Moderates, genuinely concerned about these serious topics, are being swayed by the Liberal's doomsday forecasts. But the liberal Democrats' proposed solutions are disasters in the making. Their answers inevitably involve making government bigger and the individual less responsible for his or her destiny. Enter socialism.

Here one might ask, "What does socialism have to do with any of this?" The answer is a matter of definition. Socialism centers power in the state, seeks to control business and family matters, minimizes religion, defines its own morality, and builds a bureaucracy to manage (or *mis*manage) it all. Whether or not it's intended, socialism will be the outcome if liberalism and humanism are allowed to proceed unchecked. How? Liberal politicians seeking power and control for their own sake, strive to put more everyday activities under government's control. They also push to change moral and ethical attitudes to allow for their own licentiousness. Humanists want decisions on what's right and wrong based on human reasoning, and not on tried and true faith and custom from a higher authority. Socialism views private enterprise as corruption waiting to happen and views itself as pearly white in all matters. But were socialism to rule, Americans would be reduced to a bleak subsistence-only living. The list goes on.

To continue the human body analogy, the "malignant tumor" of liberalism is putting dangerous pressure on the "organs" of our country: the family, free enterprise, security, faith, and human dignity. It's exploiting legitimate causes to a nefarious end. Don't wait until it metastasizes into full-blown socialism and America as we know it is no more.

Act now, while we are still a free nation. See through the "progressives" who are just liberals in disguise. Look beyond the "easy answer-one size fits all" rhetoric. Bring your votes to elections based on research and sound facts, not on office chatter and DJ banter.

Be informed, be responsible, be productive. Embrace goodness and be brave enough to make tough choices. That's the essence of being an American.

Special thanks to my wife C. A. Schmidt for being my sounding board and providing support, and to my editor T. S. Murley for so neatly tying my words and concepts together.

W. E. Schmidt

Order Form

For additional copies of this book, please cut or copy this order form, then fill out the following information and return with payment to the address below.

Your Name _____
Address _____
Address _____
City_____ST_____Zip_____

$15 includes shipping and handling in the U.S.
$20 outside the U.S.
Make out check or money order (no cash) to:
R. Nation
P.O. Box 834
Astor, FL 32102

For gift purchases, write the recipients' names and addresses on the back of this form.

For high volume orders and pricing, send your request in writing to the above address. Be sure to include a phone number, fax, or email address for our reply.

Note that your information will be held confidential to this transaction and will not be sold or disseminated in any way.

www.ingramcontent.com/pod-product-compliance
Lightning Source LLC
Chambersburg PA
CBHW060419290526
45791CB00002B/818